BULLIES BE GONE! PROJECT™

Comprehensive Eight-Week Course

Ages 9–17

TRAINING MANUAL FOR INSTRUCTORS,
PARENTS, AND TEACHERS

AL JOHNSON

Published by
Hybrid Global Publishing
301 E 57th Street, 4th fl
New York, NY 10022

Copyright © 2017 by Al Johnson

All rights reserved. No part of this book may be reproduced or transmitted in any form or by in any means, electronic or mechanical, including photocopying, recording, or by any information storage and retrieval system, without the written permission of the Publisher, except where permitted by law.

Manufactured in the United States of America, or in the United Kingdom when distributed elsewhere.

Johnson, Al
    Bullies Be Gone! Project: Parent/Teacher Manual

Cover design by: Joe Potter
Interior design: Claudia Volkman
Illustrations by Shanna Lim

www.bulliesbegoneproject.com

BULLIES BE GONE! PROJECT™

TO THE BULLIES BE GONE! PROJECT™ INSTRUCTORS, PARENTS, AND TEACHERS

Welcome and thank you for your interest and time in teaching our comprehensive anti-bullying program. Bullying is of major concern for children, teens, and adults. The Bullies Be Gone! Project (aka BBGP) is effective, entirely original, and unique in its approach, teaching anti-bullying skills and techniques to older children and teens, ages 9-17, and adults. You will be touching the lives of students you train in ways that will enhance their self-confidence, self-esteem, awareness, mental toughness, Language Arts learning, Common Core Requirements, and much more! Much of the training will be applicable to you as an adult.

Always keep in mind the objective of our program: *Self-Empowerment Training for Children and Teens That Prevents and Protects Against Bullying*

Students will be attending class once weekly in two (2) hour sessions for a total of 16 hours or as parents/teacher deem appropriate. (School classroom training will differ) All subject matter, for example, Lessons 3-4 or any other lesson may not be completed in one two-hour session. It is okay to have a carryover into the next week's training. Quality and understanding of skills learned by students is of high priority, rather than quantity. However, in the first 3 weeks of training, all subject matter for each class should be completed. The first three weeks are the foundation for what will be taught in the remainder of the course.

This is a comprehensive eight (8) week course, it is possible all subject matter, especially in the latter weeks, may not be covered before the completion of the course. (The training will be ongoing in the school classroom setting, not necessarily 8-weeks) Further explanation of this will be highlighted in your certification training. (Applicable if an instructor wishes to be certified to teach the course as an Independent Contractor) Each class will be different in format, and training should be based on individual growth, as opposed to competition between children in any setting.

Although the training is serious, it should be enjoyable during the learning process. Instructor enthusiasm, storytelling ability, sense of humor, teaching ability, and overall positive attitude will determine not only the content being effectively absorbed by the students, but overall student participation. There is a great deal of repetition in the training. Students are encouraged to practice BBGP's suggested guidelines in their workbook, with parent/teacher assistance for the best results.

Note: An example of how the training poems in the Bullies Be Gone! Project can effectively be used to obtain our objective is demonstrated in the very last poem My Difference Is My Strength, Lesson 8. Please refer to it NOW, then resume with Lesson 1 of the course.

Enjoy this Powerful Training Program for the Welfare of our Children and Teens, and their future!

Lesson #1
For BBGP Instructors, Parents, Teachers, Children, and Teens

Make sure children understand the concepts and objectives of each lesson to maximize the learning and retention of skills taught. Contact Al Johnson at al@antibullyingexpert.com for answers to questions you may have regarding this course.

1. **History of the program & Introductions (Instructor & Students)** (Reinforce as necessary throughout the training – The complete history of the program can be seen on the **ABOUT** page of www.antibullyingexpert.com)

The program was created by Al Johnson in 1985 in the Parks & Recreation Department of Manhattan Beach, CA. Originally, the program was called The Young, Alert, and Aware Program (YAA), a six (6) week comprehensive training, ages 5-15.
Al Johnson renamed the YAA program to The Bullies Be Gone! Project (BBGP), an eight (8) week comprehensive training, ages 9-17. Al Johnson has single-handedly taught thousands of children, teens, and adults in California these Vital Life Skills since its inception.

Objective of the Bullies Be Gone! Project Training: *Self-Empowerment Training for Children and Teens That Prevents and Protects Against Bullying*

To effectively and permanently solve a bullying problem, the child/teen must eventually or initially Eliminate or Prevent the problem independently.

2. **Instructor (Background) & Student Introductions (See website)**
3. **Physical Fitness Warm up Exercises**
4. In the eight-week comprehensive Bullies Be Gone! Project training, specific fitness exercises are taught. Being physically fit better enhances a child's/teen's ability to avoid being bullied.

    Explain Reasons Why: A fit child's self-esteem may be positively impacted; escaping from and/or controlling a bully may be easier if the child/teen is fit; successfully running from a threatening situation with a bully may be the results of being fit; and having the appearance of being physically fit along with other visual skills taught in this program may be enough to prevent a bully from ever approaching with negative intent.

    A Bullies Be Gone! Project Physical Fitness training video will be emailed to parents/teachers upon email request to Al Johnson (See address above)

5. **Instructor Asks Student/s: Their views on Bullying**

6. **Ask:** In the student's opinion, what makes someone a Bully and if they know of someone who is a Bully? Use your discretion as the parent/teacher with number of responses. This could be an important teaching moment for all parties. (Critical Discussion)

7. **Instructor begins teaching the first subject of training: AWARENESS**

    Ask the class what does Awareness mean, and what does it mean to be Aware?

    Students will give various answers and almost all of them will be correct in some way relating to **Awareness**.

    The parent/teacher should further explain what **Awareness** means. Keen Street, School, and Internet awareness are taught in this course, including role playing, and numerous effective ways **Awareness** applies to bullying.

8. **Instructor tells the students:** In our training, I will be telling you several true **Stories** relating to bullying: Our first story is about **Awareness, Thinking on Your Feet, (Explain what this is) and being Street Smart, all important elements in making sure you can effectively eliminate or prevent bullying.**

9. **Tell the story about Al Johnson at age 15** — How he had to immediately **think on his feet with awareness skills** and handle a potential threatening bullying situation, as he was walking out his front door on the way to school. He was confronted by 3 bullies. Upon the instructor's email request, a video of Al Johnson telling this story will be sent.

10. **Words, Phrases, and Stanzas in Bold Print** in the body of the poem should be **CRITICALLY DISCUSSED with students** and how they apply to Theme and Main Idea of the poem, after the reading of each poem.

11. The following **Awareness poem and illustration** is the first Instructional creative piece in the eight-week comprehensive training.

    Students will have their workbook containing all lessons of the course. Instructor should tell students to memorize **key words, phrases, stanzas, theme(s) of poems,** and even the **entire poem**. They should develop POWERFUL WORDS of responses to a bully's negative WORDS and build self-confidence and self-esteem, whether face-to-face with a bully or online. In addition to classroom activity, the students must continue to study the poems and illustrations (which may have hidden messages) at home with their parents for **recall, retention, and review.**

12. **The reading of the poem should proceed as follows:**

    First: Ask students to take a close look at the Illustration and ask them what is the illustration saying to them? Are there any hidden messages in the illustration? Instructor should determine how many responses to accept.

    Instructor then reads the entire poem first with **conviction, voice inflection, tone, attitude, believability, understanding, and determination** to demonstrate how the students must approach the reading of poems for **self-empowerment building.** Have students read along silently as the poem is being read aloud, so they can get a feel for the poem itself. A copy of each poem with illustration and vocabulary relating to the poem, will be in their training workbook for each lesson.

    Suggestion: Use as a Class Reading: Have a different student read each stanza — ask for volunteers or instructor may assign readers — or instructor may choose any method deemed appropriate for the reading(s).

    Instructor should now ask for a volunteer/s from the class (or parent ask their children) to study for memory the entire poem at home and be ready to recite it to the class (parent) next session in front of the class (parent).

    The student must not only be able to recite it, but role play the poem for interpretation purposes and how the words speak to the student, or might speak to the bully. If more than one student wants to perform the SAME poem in front of the class, **choose a maximum of 3 students for the SAME poem for a large class:** (Teacher discretion)

    Possible Class Incentive for Learning and reciting the poem in front of the class/parent:

    A trophy will be given for the BEST performance (Hold up the trophy or some other inducement) determined by the class by a silent ballot vote (Or by parent/teacher). Trophy will be presented at the end of the eight-week training. Everyone will have an opportunity to win over the length of the course. Students can perform a maximum 2 poems in a week's lesson. This process is designed to enhance the overall objective of the Bullies Be Gone! Project Training. (Teacher discretion)

AWARENESS

What is this illustration's theme and what could be the hidden message/s in the illustration?

AWARENESS

A kid's best chance of not being bullied is to be **keenly aware** of bullies long before it's too late.

Kids must know **subtle signs** a bully might reveal and what those signs could indicate.

Too often today, a kid's attention is **focused** on iPads, cell phones, and any other electronic device.

Kids are not nearly as focused on their **environment**, people in it, or **potential trouble** that could be **lurking** almost in **plain** sight.

Bullies count on kids not being aware. This makes it easy for a kid to be caught off guard.

Being caught off guard, surprised, and confused make chances of avoiding and defeating the bully very hard.

The only good thing about bullies is that they're **easily recognized**, if a kid knows what to look for. Bullies and potential ones **tend** to have **similar traits**.

They call kids names, push and shove, and want things their way. They **seldom** smile and, when **patience** is needed, the bully has none. Bullies are **ill-equipped** to **patiently wait.**

There are other **unpleasant** signs a bully has; those are just an important few.

Kids, please learn to recognize them, you'll be more aware and have a much better chance of avoiding the bully if you do.

Stay alert, stay aware, and stay away from the bully. It's what you must **effectively learn how to do.**

By sharpening your awareness skills, the outcome will be bad for the bully, and a very good one for you.

Al Johnson

AWARENESS VOCABULARY LESSON: Critically Discuss the meanings of the following words and how they are used in the stanzas of the poem: Keenly aware, subtle signs, indicate, focused, potential, lurking, tend, similar traits, seldom, patience, ill-equipped, unpleasant, effectively, outcome.

Awareness is the first of many **VITAL LIFE SKILLS** concepts children will learn in the BBGP training program. The **Theme** of the poem is **Awareness (Ask the class to tell you what the Theme of the poem is and the possible Hidden Message(s) in the illustration itself).** This will be done with all training poems and illustrations in the course.

Parent/Teacher should teach: Important **WORDS, PHRASES & STANZAS** from the body of the poem reinforcing the theme and enhancing the self-confidence and self-esteem of children/teens (These are highlighted in **Bold Print**).

Purpose of Critical Discussion with class: Clarify meaning/s of **bold print words and phrases** and their use in the **stanzas** to effectively offset the impact of **negative words** and **inappropriate actions** by bullies, and to build a **self-empowerment mindset** in children/teens.

Bullies Be Gone! Project Training Objective: *Self-Empowerment Training for Children and Teens That Prevents and Protects Against Bullying*

The Parent/Teacher should now teach the following: It is recommended you use the script as written below or you can paraphrase as you choose.

Instructor to Students:

The following powerful lesson is designed to teach you exactly what to do immediately if anyone attempts to bully you or you fear being bullied. This technique, along with many others to follow, if learned well, practiced, and retained, according to BBGP instruction, will give you a much better chance of permanently preventing or eliminating a bullying problem effectively and independently.

Instructor Reinforces with Class:

To permanently eliminate a bullying problem, you as a child or teen must know ways to effectively (On your own) solve a bullying problem or potential one via Self-Empowerment!

HITTING THE LIGHT SWITCH

What is this illustration's theme and what could be the hidden message/s in the illustration?

Parent/Teacher now reads this POEM as an Instructional Lesson:

Have the students read silently along with you, as you read aloud. (In the comprehensive BBGP program, ideal ways the child/teen should read, learn, and retain the WORDS in poems will be taught; i.e., voice inflection, tone, conviction, etc.

After the reading(s), have a student go over to the light switch in the classroom, participating as outlined in the poem. If teaching a large group of students, the instructor should go over to the light switch, while instructing students as outlined in the POEM. (Teacher discretion) This poem WILL NOT BE ONE PERFORMED BY STUDENTS IN FRONT OF THE CLASS — It can and should be practiced at home ONLY as outlined, using "The Light Switch" in the home, with parent's permission and assistance.

HITTTING "THE LIGHT SWITCH"

In this poem, you will learn how **hitting "the light switch"** could help you in a big way get rid of a bully.

Kids, **"the light switch" is in your mind**, a place where a bully cannot touch or see.

You should **only practice** this **drill** at home or with your parent or teacher, which is the proper thing to do.

Their involvement is important, so they can learn with you.

Go over to the light switch in your house; place your **index finger** on it so you can **control** it by **flicking** it back and forth or up and down.

Now, look directly at the lights you are about to make go on and off, those lights in the ceiling or at eye level. While hitting "the light switch," **concentrate, don't look all around.**

Keep your eyes **glued** to the lights as you begin to flick them on and off. Do this very quickly about five or six times.

My question to you is: "How long did it take for the lights to go on and off?" Remember, hitting "the light switch" is all about your mind.

Did the lights go on and off in a matter of seconds, is that what you would say?

You would be correct if you said no more than a second or two. You would be correct in every way.

As a kid, you might be asking, "What does this have to do with a bully? How does this help me?"

Well, I will soon explain **further**, then you will clearly see.

If a bully ever comes around wanting to **hassle** you, **immediately hit "the light switch" in your mind.**

You must do it, if **necessary**, in any bullying situation. You must do it every single time!

Just as quickly as you saw the lights go on and off, you must do the following three things with **ease**:

Relax, React, Respond as fast as the lights went on and off. The complete necessity of this drill you will soon see.

You will be taught the **Three R's** and how to apply them in the next poem's lesson, so you can perform under a **bully's pressure**, and **perform without a glitch**.

From this poem, children and teens MUST learn if a bully **hassles** them, they must immediately know how to **effectively in their mind**, hit "the light switch."

Al Johnson

HITTING "THE LGHT SWITCH" VOCABULARY LESSON: Critically Discuss the meanings of the following words and how they are used in the stanzas of the poem: Control, flicking, concentrate, glued, further, hassle, immediately, ease, glitch, necessary.

The Theme of the Poem is Hitting "The Light Switch," a **Metaphor** for children/teens to understand the importance of their **MIND** and how to effectively and immediately use the **MIND** when confronted by a bully. It is now important to go over each of the **WORDS** and **PHRASES (In BOLD PRINT)** from the body of the poem to reinforce the theme and begin to enhance the self-confidence and self-esteem of students. Critically Discuss the meaning of each of the words and how they are used in the stanzas for offsetting the **impact of negative words** and **inappropriate actions** by bullies.

Objective: *Self-Empowerment Training for Children and Teens That Prevents and Protects Against Bullying*

Meditation for Review, Recall & Retention should now be taught to the students.

Method of teaching:

Have students sit in a **Yoga (Indian Style, Legs Crossed)** position, with their backs perfectly straight, hands resting on their knees with palms up. **Ask them to totally relax.** (More will be taught about how to relax in the next BBGP Lesson.) Tell them that when you ask them to **Close Their Eyes**, they should repeat the word **Awareness (Not out loud, but only in their Minds)**.

When they have done the repeating process five (5) times with a true understanding of what **Awareness** is and how it applies to bullying, they should **open their eyes and quickly** stand, with hands behind their backs.

It does not matter who stands first, in the middle, or last. (Make sure the class understands this — they are not in competition with each other — individual growth and understanding is key.) Standing a certain way **(Hands behind their backs, as well as sitting in a Yoga position)** instills **Uniformity, Discipline, and Concentration.** (Important elements in BBGP Comprehensive Training to Eliminate & Prevent Bullying)

Immediately after the entire class has stood from the **Awareness Meditation** drill, have the class do the same with **Hitting "The Light Switch."** As the training continues with more lessons, the students will be required to do the Meditation Drill with additional techniques to **Review, Recall & Retain** subject matter taught.

Note: If a particular student takes too long to stand and the entire class is waiting, go over to the student meditating and quietly reinforce their confidence by saying something to the effect: **"Great job, you are really concentrating well. It's okay for you to stand now!"**

It is important from Lesson 1 students understand what **AWARENESS** is and how to immediately **HIT "THE LIGHT SWITCH" (In their MIND)** if confronted by a bully or anyone else causing them to immediately feel uncomfortable.

Instructors Reinforce with Class: They are to retain the meanings of the words and phrases for future clarity and understanding and, more importantly, how the WORDS & PHRASES are being used in the poem itself. (All designed to empower them to eliminate and prevent bullying.)

Also, we want to encourage children to refer to, learn, and recite the poems frequently, so **specific words, phrases, and stanzas are ingrained in their minds**. (Much like a new Rap song they hear for the first time and soon after listening repeatedly, they know all the words.)

Parent/Teacher should place great emphasis on the following:

Important Instruction to students: They are **NOT TO PLAY** with any of the techniques they learn in BBGP or to show them to anyone other than those mentioned below. Skills and Techniques learned are **NEVER** to be demonstrated in public unless it is an authentic bullying situation.

They are to enjoy learning; however, the training **IS NOT** to be shared with friends or anyone else other than parents, teachers, students who are taking the training, or BBGP instructors.

EMPHASIZE: When what they have learned and will be learning is **PLAYED WITH (Not taken seriously) and SHOWN** to their friends, the techniques **WILL NOT WORK** in an actual bullying situation. By doing so, students will have given up the **VITALLY IMPORTANT ELEMENT OF SURPRISE** in Eliminating or Preventing bullying.

THE TRAINING IS SERIOUS. IT IS CRITICAL STUDENTS UNDERSTAND THE KNOWLEDGE and TECHNIQUES LEARNED IS THEIR SECRET TO KEEP. THEY ARE ONLY TO BE USED AS INSTRUCTED FOR BEST RESULTS. If applied properly, the skills can be very Effective against a bully or anyone seeking to take negative advantage of them.

Parent/Teacher should now do the following, including mentioning what students will learn in the next lesson:

- Review Lesson 1
- **The 3R's** & How to effectively apply them in a bullying situation
- **Mental Toughness** & How it applies to bullying and its importance

END OF LESSON 1

Lesson #2
For BBGP Instructors, Parents, Teachers, Children & Teens (This will be the continuation of Lesson #1)

1. **Review Lesson 1** — Awareness & Hitting "The Light Switch"

2. **Physical Fitness** Warm Up Exercises (approx. 10–15 minutes—see video)

3. **Parent/Teacher now will ask students to share any occurrences** during the week since the last class, requiring use of what they have previously learned. Did they witness or were involved in any Bullying situations or potential ones where Awareness & Hitting "The Light Switch" came into play? If there were incidents, discuss the student's response to the incident. Offer suggestions to make the situation better if a repeated or similar incident occurs — also ask other students how they would have reacted in a similar situation. (If applicable)

4. **Have Students Recite the Awareness Poem for trophy competition. Student Voting Ballots** (Large class of students) will be collected by instructor and calculated to determine the winner, which will be announced at the end of training.

5. **Instructor introduces the 3R's in detail to students:**

    Instructor to Students: The following powerful lesson is designed to teach you exactly what to do immediately if anyone attempts to bully you or you fear being bullied. In lesson #1 you were taught about **Awareness & Hitting "The Light Switch" in your Mind** and introduced to the **3R's (Relax, React, Respond)**. Now you will be taught exactly how to use the 3R's against a bully. This technique, if learned well, practiced, and retained, will give you a much better chance of eliminating or preventing a bullying problem permanently!

6. The following drill is an introduction to the 3R's without the class having a clue this is taking place: (Large class of students or parents can be creative at home)

Ask the class: Would everyone STAND for me now! The class will stand usually in a very methodical manner, some slower than others. Tell the class almost immediately after everyone stands, you may now sit back down. I will explain.

Now Ask the Class: (How many of you know what **PUSH-UPS** are?) You will see almost all hands up — instructor should now demonstrate doing a few push-ups.

Instructor now tells Class: When I first asked you to stand, you stood with **no real purpose in mind**, you just stood up as you would **NORMALLY STAND**. And that was just fine.

However, I'm going to ask you to stand again, this time you **MUST NOT** be the last one to stand. **Repeat with Emphasis: YOU MUST NOT BE THE LAST ONE TO STAND!** I will be looking carefully for the last person who stands. If you are that person, the last one, you are going to have to come up front with me and do **(Hesitate) 100 PUSH-UPS. (This drill may not apply to the older teen age group — Teacher Discretion)**

Your parents are going to wonder where suddenly you developed so many muscles. You will also be very sore from doing 100 PUSH UPS. **SO, DO NOT BE THE LAST ONE TO STAND!** Watch the class closely, some will try to get a head start by not being completely seated in the "Yoga position." Make sure they are all seated correctly before asking them to stand.

Upon your signal, direct the class in an **EXCITED VOICE: DON'T BE THE LAST ONE TO STAND WHEN I GIVE YOU THE SIGNAL: (Hesitate) EVERYBODY STAND!!** Of course, there will be a kid who obviously stands last and maybe another kid will point to that kid. Immediately tell the pointing kid/s they are not to be concerned with anyone else in the class but themselves. (A teaching moment) And of course, **NO ONE DOES PUSH-UPS!**

Tell the class: Guess what? Without you even knowing it, you just performed the 3R's, which you must immediately do after Hitting "The Light Switch" in your mind if a **Bully** ever gets in your face in a threatening manner.

Here are the 3R's again, and you **MUST NOT** ever forget them, **EVER, FOR THE REST OF YOUR LIFE!** You will be tested later in this training to see if you know what the 3R's are and how to apply them, as well as other skills you will be learning.

Have the class repeat the 3R's one at a time with **enthusiasm** and **conviction**. Use a phrase something to the effect:

Instructor to Students: I want to feel this building shake, when you repeat each of the 3R's. Instructor repeats each one first, then the class repeats after. If the instructor is not satisfied with the class' response, have them repeat again.

RELAX, REACT, RESPOND

What is this illustration's theme and what could be the hidden message/s in the illustration?

Just as in Lesson #1 — The reading of this POEM is for Instructional purposes as the class receives the explanation of the 3R's — Instructor reads the poem as the 3R's are being taught. **The underlined is not a part of the poem.** These are instructions to enhance the necessary training of the 3R's after certain stanzas.

RELAX, REACT, RESPOND

Okay, class, in the poem before this one you learned about hitting "the light switch" in your mind to help you defeat the bully, if you have to.

I introduced the Three R's, now you're going to learn what they mean and how to put them to good use.

Relax is the first thing you must do if the bully ever gets in your face. "So, how do I relax," you might say?

Take a quick, quiet, deep breath, inhale and suck the air in through your nose, exhale, quietly blow the air out through your mouth quickly. Do it two or three times.

<u>**Demonstrate and have the class perform relaxation while they are sitting.**</u>

Imagine you are pinching a balloon that you just blew air into between your thumb and index finger to keep the air inside.

<u>**I actually use a balloon to demonstrate — blow it up, pinch it, then quickly let the air out.**</u>

As soon as you take your finger and thumb away, the air rushes out, the balloon goes limp and becomes very relaxed.

By relaxing quickly in a bad situation, especially with a bully, your muscles don't become tense and your mind remains clear, now you can better react.

<u>**Instructor demonstrates what tense muscles look like.**</u>

React is to immediately decide how you are going to allow yourself to feel about this unwanted bully situation. Proper relaxation should help you take control.

You will either feel scared or excited, very aware or unaware of your surroundings, confident or not confident, ready or not ready to immediately take control.

<u>**Instructor emphasizes if the student does feel excited and scared, they must do so in a controlled fashion — instructor demonstrates a non-controlling scared, excited reaction.**</u>

You will react in pretty much one of these ways.

Now you must decide how you are going to **Respond**. Your goal is to cause the bully to have a very bad day.

Here are ways you can **Respond**: walk away from the bully as fast as you can, it may or may not be the best solution, and the bully may follow you.

Demonstrate the incorrect and correct ways to walk away from the bully:

Incorrect Way: By the kid immediately turning his/her back to the bully to walk away, where the bully is in physical striking distance as the kid's back is turned.

Correct Way: Now demonstrate cautiously walking away from the bully, the kid never fully turns his/her back until they are a safe distance away. Role play this with the students.

Run away from the bully as fast as you can, with your purpose being to find a **responsible** adult to help you.

However, unless you've been taught **"Emergency Running Skills,"** this may or may not be a wise thing for you to do.

Instructor informs class they will be taught these running skills later in their training.

The bully could possibly chase and catch you.

If you are caught, the bully is probably angry, and could get physical with you. Unless you've been trained in proper self-defense and self-confidence skills, this move would be an advantage for the bully, not for you.

Instructor informs class they will be taught Controlling & Escaping Self-Defense skills later in the course.

If you have the confidence, you can try to talk your way out of the situation. If you choose this response, you must be stone-faced and look the bully straight in the eyes.

Role play this scenario with volunteers from the class. (If applicable) I usually have a kid come up and grab me with one on two hands, much like a bully would do, as I'm on my knees. The kid volunteering is the Bully and I'm the victim, then we reverse roles.

The instructor should then go around to each kid in the class individually and grab them in a similar fashion. Each student in the class must pass the stone-faced-look-in-the-eyes-of-the-bully test to successfully complete this section of training.

If the bully is demanding you give him/her something of yours, you can choose to do so or not. If the bully has a weapon, give them what they want, you must quickly comply.

If the bully has no weapon and he/she decides to get physical with you,

Your last reaction, because you have no other choice, is to get physical, too.

However, to fend off a bully physically may require certain self-defense skills, especially ones where punches are not thrown, but the bully is put under your physical control.

Inform the class, they will learn Controlling and Escaping techniques from a bully, in future lessons.

You will need specific training to learn these skills so your reaction can be brave and bold.

Relax, React, Respond must be done by you just as fast as the lights went on and off when you were hitting "the light switch."

You'll need and receive from this class special training and practice to effectively Relax, React, and Respond in an uncomfortable bully situation, how to do so, and hopefully, without a glitch.

Al Johnson

Remind the class: You performed the 3R's with a **PURPOSE** when you were first asked to not be the last one standing and you didn't even know you were doing it. Your response was **INSTINCTIVE. (Explain to the class an INSTINCTIVE RESPONSE or first ask for a definition from student/s)**

That is exactly what you must **immediately** do if a Bully ever gets in your face trying to intimidate you: **Awareness, Hitting "The Light Switch," and applying the 3R's, Relax, React, Respond, all must be done in a matter of seconds!**

The Instructor Must: Go over each of the following words contained in the 3R's poem with the class for enhanced understanding and clarity:

THE 3R's VOCABULARY LESSON: Inhale, exhale, limp, tense, control, immediately, stone-faced, comply, brave, bold, relax, react, respond, fend, glitch, effectively

Go over the **PHRASES and WORDS of the poem IN BOLD PRINT** and **Critically Discuss** how they apply to the theme of the poem.

Ask the Students: What Relax, React, Respond "without a glitch" means to them

Introduce: MENTAL TOUGHNESS LESSON

Instructor Informs Class: The following important lesson is designed to help you begin understanding **the power of your Mind and how you must develop Toughness of the Mind to Defeat Bullies.** The bully uses **nasty words** to destroy your self-confidence, self-esteem, and weaken your mind. This occurs face-to-face or online. If the bully is successful in bullying you, you could have unpleasant and unhealthy thoughts lasting for a very long time.

Specific Words and Actions can empower you and weaken the bully's negative hold on you. I want the bully to clearly see you as no longer a victim or potential one. You're going to be **mentally tough** and display **EMPOWERED Self-Confidence and Self-Esteem a bully CANNOT penetrate or deflate. YOU MUST BELIEVE THAT YOU ARE EMPOWERED** and continue to become even mentally stronger. **(Explain to class CONVICTION of BELIEF, as necessary)**

Instructor tells class the following True Story (All stories in BBGP told to students are actual events):

Instructor should request via email the actual video of Al Johnson telling this story

Instructor tells the story about a 13-year-old girl walking home in broad daylight, passing through a closed car wash and how she UNFORTUNATELY FAILED TO practice Awareness, Hitting "The Light Switch" or the 3R's and was taken advantage of.

This story applies greatly today, where children, teens, and adults walking from point A to B, are keenly aware of their I-Phones and other devices, BUT NOT ADEQUATELY AWARE OF THEIR ENVIRONMENT!

Instruction & Class Exercise:

Have the class now practice this drill to help instill **MENTAL TOUGHNESS:**

Have the class quickly stand. Remind them **every time** in the future, they are asked to stand or sit in the training, they are to do so as if they **DO NOT** want to be the last one to stand, performing Awareness, Hitting "The Light Switch," and the 3R's every single time.

Class Mental Toughness Training:

Students should repeat 5 times, as the instructor counts, the inhale, exhale relaxation drill with their arms and each time. (This method was demonstrated on the physical fitness video)

- They are to **lip sync (with eyes closed) "I am mentally tough,"** the very last time, **(#5)** have them do the same breathing drill, however, they do not lip sync the phrase, but **open their eyes**, pretending they are looking a bully straight in the eyes, stoned-faced, as they say out loud, **"I am mentally tough."**
- At instructor's discretion, the class can orally state a few more times, with the inhale, exhale relaxation drill, **"I am mentally tough."**

Instructor reinforces Mentally Tough in the following manner or Paraphrase: For the rest of your life, no matter the circumstance, never forget that you are and must be **MENTALLY TOUGH!**

Instructor continues: NO ONE can take your **Mental Toughness** away from you unless you ALLOW THEM TO DO SO! AND YOU ARE NOT GOING TO ALLOW THAT TO HAPPEN!

Instructor can reinforce this training: With any mental toughness situations the instructor has encountered. Also explain how some athletes are MENTALLY TOUGHER than others. And explain how MENTAL TOUGHNESS can be of great benefit in their ACADEMICS at school.

Instruct Students: This technique, if learned well and retained, will give you a much better chance of preventing and eliminating a bully problem permanently. You must follow and practice the instructions taught in this course.

Instruct Students, they should continue to: Study the poems, even memorize specific powerful words, stanzas and the entire poem. By doing so, students will become **EMPOWERED** and the Bully will become weaker and ineffective in their eyes and more importantly, in their mind.

Each poem contains WORDS & PHRASES to empower, send powerful defeating messages to bullies, and powerful messages for bullies to **IMMEDIATELY CEASE THEIR INAPPROPRIATE BEHAVIOR.**

Make sure children and teens understand the Main Idea or Theme of each poem.

Instruct Students: Discuss the poem with their parents, expressing their point of view of the poem, and ask parents for theirs. Everyone learns by doing so.

Instruct Students: Study the illustration of each poem carefully before and after reading the poem. There may be hidden messages in each illustration, some that come to mind after reading the poem.

Students Should Enjoy: Learning skills and techniques to help develop effective ways of eliminating or preventing a bully problem permanently without anyone's help via **Self-Empowerment!!**

Instructor Informs Students: As you read the poem, imagine you are talking directly to the bully with the words in the poem. If you ever must say them to a bully, I want you to develop the confidence to do so, if you don't have it now. If your confidence is already strong, I want the **WORDS** you learn in all the Bullies Be Gone! Project lessons, to make you even mentally stronger and more confident.

Instructor Reminds Class: Whenever speaking directly to a bully face to face, no matter how difficult it is to do, **YOU MUST look the bully straight in the eyes with your stone-faced (but relaxed) expression, just as we practiced.**

If the bullying is on the Internet, and you're responding to NEGATIVE WORDS by a bully directed at you, you're going to **COPY & PASTE WORDS or PHRASES** from specific poems that apply from your Bullies Be Gone! Project Poetry book and training workbook.

While pasting, you are to imagine that you are face to face with the bully, looking the bully straight in the eyes as you are pasting your powerful response. Your computer screen is the eyes of the bully!

My Mental Toughness

What is this illustration's theme and what could be the hidden message/s in the illustration?

MY MENTAL TOUGHNESS

My mental toughness wasn't anywhere to be found when you started bullying me.

I didn't think much of myself; your bullying made me feel small and weak.

I spent a lot of time being angry and crying. I didn't laugh like before, not very much at all.

You were winning, and what little pride I had left was sinking fast. I felt like banging my head against the wall.

Then my parents told me that bullies might be physically strong, but mentally they are very weak.

They told me to develop my mental toughness, and by doing so, I could easily defeat the bully.

So, I started thinking and really believing I was strong, in body and mind.

And you know what? The more I thought about being mentally tough, the more confidence I seemed to find.

Mental toughness is a powerful tool that all kids should develop, have, and constantly use.

If a bully happens to come into your space, the bully will see, sense, and feel your mental toughness. The bully will know if he/she tries bullying you, they cannot win, no way! The bully is destined to lose.

Al Johnson

MENTAL TOUGHNESS VOCABULARY LESSON: Pride, sinking, develop, constantly, sense, destined – ask the class what the words mean and discuss how the words relate to the theme of the poem.

Have the Class Explain the Phrase and Question: Physically Strong, but Mentally Weak & What does being Mentally Tough mean?

LESSON 2 SUMMARY:

Meditation for Review, Recall & Retention

Method of teaching:

Have student(s) sit in a Yoga (Indian Style) position, with their back(s) perfectly straight, hands resting on knees, with palms up. Tell students to totally relax. When you ask them to **Close Their Eyes**, you want them to repeat (Not out loud, but only in their Minds) Awareness, Hitting "The Light Switch," Relax, React, Respond, & Mental Toughness. They will be sitting and standing for each concept as previously taught in the Meditation section at the end of Lesson 1.

When they complete the repeating process five (5) times for each **Key Concept** with a true understanding how they apply to bullying, they should open their eyes and quickly stand, hands behind their backs. (like hands behind the back when someone is being handcuffed) It is paramount students understand the CONCEPTS taught in the first 2 Lessons.

This process will be repeated at the end of each week's lesson. **(However, because of comprehensive course content, meditation at the end of each Lesson will be at the discretion of the instructor, but highly recommended)** Each week the class will have more concepts to Mentally Review, Recall, and Retain.

Instructor Informs Class: To practice this Mental Retention Drill at least 3 times a week on their own before the next class session.

Inform the students again, they are to retain the meanings of the words for future clarity and understanding and more importantly, how the **WORDS** are being used in the poem itself. (All designed to empower them to defeat and prevent Bullying)

Again Encourage Students: to learn and recite the poems frequently, so specific words, phrases, stanzas, and the poem itself are automatically ingrained in their minds.

Reinforce with Students:
They are **NOT to PLAY** with any of the techniques they learn in BBGP or display them **IN PUBLIC**. The training **IS NOT** to be shared with friends (Unless it is a friend who is enrolled in the BBGP course) or anyone else other than parents, teachers, or BBGP instructors.

Students should be instructed to practice all techniques they have been taught at least 3 times during the week, re-read the poems for retention, clarity, understanding, and **SELF-EMPOWERMENT.**

EMPHASIZE: When techniques in the BBGP training are **PLAYED WITH and SHOWN** to friends or other kids, the techniques **WILL NOT WORK** against a real life bully situation. By doing so, students will have given up the **KEY ELEMENT OF SURPRISE** in eliminating or preventing bullying.

The training should be taken seriously and enjoyable to learn to be effective in eliminating and preventing bullying.

Instructor introduces Next Week's Training:

- Body Language (How it applies to Bullying)
- SIC (How it applies to Bullying)
- Street Smart Awareness Training & Bullying Prevention
- Cyberspace Online Bullying (Ways to eliminate, prevent, and respond to it)

END OF LESSON 2 — (This realistically could be the 2nd and 3rd weeks of BBGP training, depending on class progression and instructor discretion. There could be carry-over of training from lesson to lesson. Previous Lesson's content should be reviewed before a new lesson is taught.

Lessons 3 & 4
For BBGP Instructors, Parents, Children & Teens
Children & Teens (This will be the continuation of Lesson #1 & 2.)

Physical Fitness Warm Up Exercises (approx. 10-15 minutes – see original video, as necessary)

Reinforce and Review: Awareness, Hitting "The Light Switch," The 3R's, & Mental Toughness, and their importance in BBGP training

Ask students to share any occurrences since the last class requiring the use of their BBGP skills. Did they witness or were involved in any Bullying situations or potential ones? (If there were incidents, discuss with students, offer suggestions to make the situation better if repeated, or if similar incidents occur)

Instructor to Students: Specific Words and phrases can empower you and weaken the bully's negative hold on you. I want the bully to clearly see you as no longer being the victim or potential one. You are going to be keenly aware and mentally tough, possessing **POWERFUL Self-Confidence and Self-Esteem** a bully cannot **Defeat, Deflate,** or **Take Away** from you. **HOWEVER, YOU MUST ALWAYS BELIEVE, DISPLAY & PRACTICE THIS WITH CONVICTION. (Your Mental Toughness)**

These skills, if learned well and retained, will give you a much better chance of eliminating or preventing a bullying problem permanently.

Remind the Class: They should continue to do the following with this lesson and lessons that follow:

- Study the poem, even memorize the poem for their empowerment and the bully's weakness. Each poem contains words and phrases to empower and send powerful messages to bullies to cease their inappropriate behavior.

- Make sure you understand the **main idea or theme** of each poem. Discuss the poem with your parents/teachers, express your point of view of the poem and ask your parents to express theirs. With this process, everyone learns.

Instructor to Students: Study the illustration of each poem carefully before and after you read the poem. There may be hidden messages in each illustration. What specifically is the illustration saying to you and what does it say to your parents or teacher? See if your parents/teachers see what you see in the illustration. (Critically Discuss)

Learning BBGP skills and techniques are to help you develop effective ways of eliminating or preventing a bullying problem permanently. For this to occur, you must learn, practice, and retain the **empowering messages** sent with these *poetic words & phrases.*

Instructor should repeat this often to the students during the training.

As you read the poem, imagine you are talking directly to the bully with the WORDS in the poem. If it becomes necessary to say them face to face to a bully, I want you to develop the confidence to do so with conviction. If your confidence is already strong, I want the **WORDS** you learn in all the Bullies Be Gone! Project lessons to make you **mentally stronger and more confident.**

Instructor will now introduce: SIC and how it applies to Bullying, Awareness, The 3R's, Hitting The Light Switch, and Mental Toughness.

Instructor to Students: In an uncomfortable emergency, especially with a Bully or someone trying to take advantage of you **mentally or physically,** three (3) factors almost always come into play:

- These three (3) factors are the acronym **SIC** (Pronounced 'Sick')

Ask Class: Do you have an idea what the S stands for, (wait for a response for each letter) the I, and then the C — **After you receive answers from the class, explain SIC, as necessary. You may get some correct responses, not likely for all 3 letters:**

- **SIC = Surprise, Intimidation, Confusion**
- **Instructor reinforces the story of — previous video of Al Johnson telling the story:** A 13-year-old young lady walking home across a car wash in broad daylight and was approached by a man seeking to do her harm, and how **SIC** certainly came into play — **Instructor demonstrates** — This incident was shown on the news, unfortunately the girl became a victim.

If the class is comprised of children, ages 9-10, **do not** go into any details of the abduction. If the children are older, discuss more if questions arise regarding the outcome of the incident. (However, stay away from graphic details — the girl was sexually molested and killed.)

- **Explain to Class:** If they are ever in a threatening situation of any nature, especially with a Bully, **they must apply 2 elements of SIC** and immediately put into action, Awareness, Hitting "The Light Switch," 3R's, Body Language, and Mental Toughness, all in a matter of a few seconds (Yes, it can be done with the training the students are receiving. These skills will be taught throughout the training)

- **Ask Class:** If they know what the 2 elements of **SIC** they should immediately apply are? (Wait for a response)
- **They are: S=Surprise, C=Confusion**
- **I = Intimidation** should be used ONLY when **Physical Controlling** or **Escaping** techniques are used (Inform the class, these skills will be taught later in the training)
- **Tell Students:** They must reverse SIC a bully automatically applies, by DOING THE UNEXPECTED. Bullies DO NOT like THE ELEMENT OF SURPRISE & CONFUSION (Bullies do not enjoy being intimidated either)

Instructor Introduces Body Language Instruction:

- **Ask Class:** To stand in their normal standing position, which they will automatically do. (Reinforce not being the last one to stand, as practiced in the 3R's training) The class has no clue as to what is about to take place.
- **Instructor will Conduct Body Language Inspection by:** Going around the room, stopping briefly in front of each student, and looking them up and down, much like the military.

Instructor informs students before inspection: If I tap you on the shoulder, you may immediately sit in the cross-legged position. (Yoga style) If I pass you by without tapping you on the shoulder or tell you to sit, you are **TO REMAIN STANDING**.

- **The Instructor:** Is looking at each student's **BODY LANGUAGE** as they stand in front of them for a second or so. Is their body language poor, need improving, or just plain bad? These are the students who will remain standing. If their body language is excellent or good, these are the students who will be told to sit or tapped on the shoulder. **The class remains unaware of the purpose of this training.**
- Do not embarrass student(s) who remain standing: Say something to the effect: Those of you who are still standing are probably wondering why? I will now explain. Please, you may have a seat. Everyone is now sitting.
- **Instructor to Students:** What I was taking a close look at was your **BODY LANGUAGE** (Have the students repeat 2 or 3 times with conviction, **BODY LANGUAGE**)

Those of you I instructed to sit, your body language was good. in fact, a few of you had **EXCELLENT BODY LANGUAGE** (point them out for the class. Have them stand again for the class to see their excellent body language.

- **Instructor to Students:** This is **NOT A CRITICISM**, so don't be embarrassed, those of you who were left standing, your **BODY LANGUAGE** was not as **STRONG** and **CONFIDENT** as it needs to be. But we will correct that. In fact, we will improve everyone's body language, which will give you another effective tool to defeat a bully or prevent one from approaching you.
- **Instructor Explains:** Why **BODY LANGUAGE** is so very important in relations to being approached or not approached in an uncomfortable manner by a Bully or anyone else. (Refer to Al Johnson's video of Body Language stories and of course instructor's knowledge of the subject matter)

Tell the following 2 stories related to Body Language (See video of Al Johnson demonstrating the following — Instructor should request video via Email):

1. Al Johnson being at the police station, seeing and hearing a middle-aged man being interrogated **(I usually ask the Class to define Interrogate)** who had been in and out of jail most of his life for committing crimes against children & teens **(Body Language related, along with class volunteer/s and Role Play — see video)**

2. Al Johnson strolling through the mall while being watched (unknowingly) by a lady in the mall and what she said to Al as he came abreast of her **(Body Language related, see video)**

Teacher should now ask for 4 volunteers from the class (If applicable) — Each volunteer will go to a different corner of the class. (4 corners) The class will be instructed to watch carefully the body language of each student as they individually walk completely around the class, back to where they started from. The class will grade their individual body language while walking. (Oral evaluations) Parents at home can do the same drill as they deem appropriate in the house, outside, at a park, etc.

Purpose: How are students evaluating their peers' body language? Good, outstanding, ok, could use improvement, etc. Inform the class how important **constructive criticism** is and the fact the **Bully** is seeing the same body language as the class, teachers, or parents saw.

After this drill is over, Instructor says to class (Paraphrase as needed): Your body language and how you appear to others could be the difference in a bully or anyone else approaching you with bad intent or deciding not to approach because of the powerful signal your body is sending to the Universe. **We want that to be Your Magnificent & Self-Confident Body Language.**

Instructor to Students: Practice having good or excellent body language for the rest of your life. Students can sometimes even help their parents/teachers with the importance of adult body language. Often adults are not as aware of their body language as they should be. (Especially with the today's attention-grabbing electronic devices everyone seems to have)

Another story follows to help children/teens mentally remember, develop and maintain Good Body Language for the rest of their lives:

Tell the story: About a 12-year-old girl on stage with Al Johnson and how Al immediately improved the girl's body language from poor to confident and powerful. Instruct the class that they must do the same with the **"Name of Their Street Drill"** and how it applies to them. **(Role Play with a student volunteer — see video by Al Johnson)**

BODY LANGUAGE

What is this illustration's theme and what could be the hidden message/s in the illustration?

BODY LANGUAGE

Kids, your body language says a lot about you.

It tells the world if you have **confidence or not** in almost everything you do.

If your shoulders are **drooping** and you appear to always be looking at the ground,

A bully will surely see your poor body language, and quickly decide you're the perfect kid to **hound**.

You must stand tall, walk with your chin up and shoulders back. You'll be telling the world you are a kid that is alert and aware.

<u>**Instructor Reminds Class: This is tough to do on a consistent basis in today's society with kids and adults walking with their eyes glued to an electronic device – discuss with the class the dangers of constantly doing this and how it gives the bully and the bad person the advantage.)**</u>

The bully will take one long look at you and **quickly conclude** you're not someone to be picked on at all. The best choice for the bully will be to go elsewhere.

Be proud of who you are each and every day and **display it from head to toe.**

Your good body language will be a powerful tool for you to use. It may be all you need to prevent the bully from coming anywhere close.

Al Johnson

<u>**Tell the Story (See video by Al Johnson):**</u> <u>About a lady walking with a baby strapped to the front of her body while her eyes were glued to the iPhone in her hand and how she was taken advantage of. (Request Video of Al Johnson telling the story)</u>

BODY LANGUAGE VOCABULARY: Drooping, hound, conclude, display, prevent

Instructor Introduces: Being Street Smart & How It Applies to Bullying:

What Does Being Street Smart Mean?

- First and foremost, it's being keenly aware of your environment always — at school, at play, in the park, with your parents, the mall, etc.
- **Use mall scenario, gun fire breaks out drill, teach the drop, spread eagle, military crawl. This training will have a great deal of class role playing and involvement.** (See video by Al Johnson — All videos must be requested by instructor via email. A link to the video will be sent via email)
- **Teach this gun situation:** On the street when someone attempts to force a child or teen into a vehicle at gunpoint **(Video by Al Johnson)** Six & eleven-year-old brothers playing in an alley and how a gun was involved **(Class Role Playing will be a part of this training (See video above)**
- **Tell the Story:** Resident in the neighborhood across from an elementary school firing on a campus full of children and what transpired (Class Role Playing will be a part of this training) (See video by Al Johnson)

Role Playing in BBGP training is designed to enhance the chances of children and teens Eliminating & Preventing Bullying

Students should **Anticipate Trouble or a possible Bully Situation** before it occurs. Being Mentally Tough always helps the child/teen immediately apply Awareness, Hitting "The Light Switch," the 3R's, and Body Language as a **Reflective Reaction (Instructor explains Reflective Reaction to the class, as necessary)** in a possible uncomfortable situation.

- These skills critically apply to children/teens knowing effective methods and techniques of how to **"Think on Their Feet"** in an emergency or uncomfortable Bullying situation.

Introduce Street Awareness Scenarios Training

Explain to Class: At some point in time, if not currently, a child or teen will be walking from point A to point B without adult supervision. **Bullies come in all ages, skin colors, shapes, and sizes**, looking for an opportunity to take advantage of anyone they can. Keen Street Awareness is a VITAL LIFE SKILL that we all MUST have and effectively apply, no matter our age.

Today's Street Awareness Lesson: (See Al Johnson instruct on video)

Take two (2) chairs representing two cars going in opposite directions.

With this lesson, you want to teach: (See same video above)

The Safer Side of the Street to Walk on and Why — Demonstrate what could and has happened to children walking on the side of the street that gives the Bully and/or Predator an advantage.

Role Play: Safer side of the street to walk on with class volunteers and what to do if being threatened or followed and how to draw attention to the situation — picking up an available **BLUNT OBJECT** and what to do with it comes into play — **Creating an imaginary friendly person or relative** comes into play **(See video above)**

Instructors Introduces Blind Spot and Street Safety — Role Play with the class (All demonstrated in the same video above)

Choose a class volunteer: (If applicable) Show how he/she would walk on the street, for example, from 20th to 25th Street, to their destination. The child/teen is alone, but could also be with friends. **Role Play**

The child/teen above is about 5 blocks or more from his/her destination. Suddenly, out of nowhere, someone appears from behind. The strange person makes the child feel uncomfortable by aggressively yelling out: i.e., "Hey kid come here for a second, I want to show you this." "You really need to see this. Kids love this, just take a minute, you'll be glad you did, come here!" **(Or anything aggressive, yet enticing, making the child feel uncomfortable, but maybe curious)**

Tell the Story: (See video by Al Johnson) About how Al Johnson used an enticing trick in a street situation against a 12-year-old boy as a test

Reinforce how Awareness, Hitting "the light switch," the 3R's, SIC, Mental Toughness, and Body Language all play an important role in these Street Safety Awareness situations.

Teach what the child must YELL if he/she wants attention drawn to them in an emergency street or real life dangerous situation and why.

Ask the class: If they were in trouble with someone threatening them and they wanted attention drawn to their threatening situation, what would they yell?

The word **"FIRE"** should be yelled more than the word **"HELP"** — e.g., fire, fire, fire, fire, help, help, fire! Most of the class will not know to yell **"FIRE"** in an emergency. Maybe explain to the class why yelling **"FIRE"** for instance, in a "movie theatre," when there is no actual fire, is unlawful.

Tell the Story (Al Johnson is telling the story on video): About a 17-year-old high school girl who was sexually assaulted by a gang of boys and how neighbors responded to her as the neighbors heard her yell for **HELP! This incident was on the News.**

BEING STREET-SMART

What is this illustration's theme and what could be the hidden message/s in the illustration?

BEING STREET-SMART

You may be asking yourself, **"What does being street-smart mean and what does that have to do with me?"**

Almost all kids are **sheltered** and **protected** by their parents or other responsible adults, and that's how it should be.

When a bully **hassles** another kid, that kid is no longer under the **protective umbrella** of parents or responsible adults. The kid is left to fend for him/herself all too often, eventually in the **mean streets**.

If a kid is not street-smart, and most are not, **the bully has the advantage.** The bully is then tough to defeat.

Being street-smart is **being confident, alert, aware, and having the ability to create confusion and doubt in the bully's mind.**

This is not easily done when a kid has been sheltered all the time.

Being street-smart is **knowing words to say, things to do, and not do** when a bully has decided he/she wants to bully you.

Being street-smart is doing exactly what a bully doesn't expect you to do.

Bullies carefully avoid street-smart kids, so make sure the bully quickly knows to stay away from you.

Street-smart kids create on the fly, as quickly as can be.

A street-smart kid's antennae are sharply tuned for any negative possibility.

Street-smart kids quickly reverse a bully situation in their favor. A kid must be trained to be street-smart by someone who knows and understands the streets.

It may or may not be the parents who do the training; however, **what a kid wants to avoid, is for the street-smart training to come from the bully.**

Al Johnson

Students should now volunteer to compete in the Awareness Poem for next week's performance — maximum of 3 students chosen. (If applicable)

STREET SMART VOCABULARY: Sheltered, protected, protective umbrella, fend, avoid, create on the fly, antennae, sharply tuned

Critically Discuss with Class: Words, phrases, and stanzas in bold print for their meanings and overall importance regarding the Theme and Main Idea of the poem

Instructor to Students: You have just completed your 4th Lesson in the Bullies Be Gone! Project Training Program. Let's now evaluate how much you have learned and, more importantly, how well you have retained the information.

END OF LESSONS #3 & #4 — No meditation or revise, recall, retention drills for this class, unless instructor chooses to do so — instructor reminds students to practice as before.

Instructor to Students: Answer the following questions to the quiz with your best responses. Give your completed quiz to your parents, if being trained at home or to your teacher. Make sure your responses and answers are entirely yours.

Your quiz will be graded by your parent, teacher, or our staff, if you are taking the course online. Upon successful completion of the entire Bullies Be Gone Comprehensive Course, you will be awarded a Certificate of Completion, along with a Bonus Gift.

Bullies Be Gone Retention Quiz — Lessons 1–4

Students have access to this Quiz in their workbook where they can write their answers directly or on a separate sheet of paper to prevent tearing out the pages of the workbook. Parents and Teachers are encouraged to take this same quiz. Comparing answers with students can be a FUN learning experience.

Your Name: _____ Age_____

1. **Hitting "The Light Switch"** is all about a child's or teen's what?

2. Explain how using the Hitting "The Light Switch" technique could prevent you from being bullied or help eliminate a bullying problem you might have.

3. What are **the 3R's** and in what specific order should they take place?

R_____   R_____   R_____

4. Explain what happens with each of the 3R's and why knowing the proper use of each one could help you prevent being bullied or eliminate a problem you currently may be having with a bully.

R_____

_____

R_____

_____

R_____

5. What does it mean to be **Mentally Tough** and why is it important for a child/teen to have Mental Toughness to defeat the bully or prevent being bullied. And to be mentally tough, no matter what age a person happens to be?

6. Children and Teens who are keenly _____ and know how bullies act and carry themselves stand a much better chance of not being bullied. (Fill in the blank with the correct word to complete the statement.)

Why did you answer the way you did in #6? Explain in the space below:

7. What does **Good Body Language** have to do with keeping a bully or bad person away from you and how you appear to the world around you?

8. How would you describe good body language? How would you describe poor or bad body language?

Good Body Language

Poor or Bad Body Language

9. What message(s) do you get from the **Awareness Illustration**? & What is the theme or main idea of the poem?

10. What message(s) do you get from the **Body Language Illustration?** & What is the theme or main idea of the Body Language poem?

Bring your complete Quiz next week to class with all your answers. (If applicable) or mail your Quiz with answers to Al Johnson: al@antibullyingexpert.com.

Children, teens, and adults should test their knowledge of the first 4 lessons by the answers to this quiz. There will be 10 points given for each correct response for a total of 100 points.

Partially correct answers get 5 points and incorrect answers get zero. **A total score less than 75 require re-studying lesson 1-4**, and resending a new completed Quiz. To qualify for the Certificate of Completion and the Bonus Prize, a minimum score of 75 must be attained on every Quiz.

Contact Al Johnson or Bullies Be Gone! Project instructor via email address above for answers to any questions.

Learning and Retaining the BBGP Vital Life Skills Training of each lesson is mandatory for a child or teen. By doing so, their chances of effectively Eliminating or Preventing a bullying problem should be enhanced.

Lessons 5-6 — For BBGP Instructors, Parents, Teachers, Children & Teens — Cyberspace Bullying — A Real Epidemic in Our Society

- **Discuss any events** that occurred with the children since the last class that involved a Bullying situation or a potential one.
- **Physical Fitness Training**
- **Student Class Performances for Trophy consideration from last week's poem(s) chosen (If Applicable)**
- **Briefly review important points** covered in previous lessons — Students should have received back graded quizzes and/or homework from parent, teacher, or Al Johnson via email.

Instructor to Students: The following important lessons are specifically designed to help you learn effective methods of **defeating, deflecting, and nullifying the effects of a bully's negative impact.**

Intended Results: Rendering insignificant A BULLY'S HATEFUL WORDS & NASTY RUMORS ONLINE.

Instructor Informs Class: These skills & techniques (Online training) CAN & SHOULD be suggested to a close friend who may be having an ONLINE BULLYING PROBLEM

You will now begin to understand ways to develop skills and **POWERFUL WORDS** to defeat the bully's **online inappropriate intent.**

You will learn to do this with **EMPOWERING CONFIDENCE & CONVICTION.** The six (6) poetic and powerful lessons we are now going to thoroughly cover are: **Hateful Words, Rumors On Line, You Hide In Front Of A Computer, Social Skills Too, Social Network Caution & The Stranger On The Internet**

WORDS CAN: *Deflate, Harm, Hurt, & Unfortunately, Kill*

WORDS CAN: *Empower, Build Self-Confidence, Inspire, Motivate & Heal*
These are exactly what **WORDS** in the Bullies Be Gone! Project are designed to do.

Instructor to Students:

If you understand as a child or teen, or even an adult, when confronted with a Bullying situation:

- Specific Words to say
- How to say them (Effectively with Conviction)
- When and When not to say them
- What actions to take after saying them
- When and how to take them

You will be better positioned effectively to fend off rumors online and the negative affect such rumors can have on your self-confidence and self-esteem. You will begin to know or enhance understanding the importance of who you really are as a person, and pride you should always display and have, no matter what anyone says negatively about you.

Instructor States Emphatically to Students: <u>*"WHAT SOMEONE SAYS ABOUT YOU OR TO YOU, NO MATTER HOW HATEFUL OR NASTY IT IS, SHOULD NOT BE TO THE DETRIMENT OF HOW YOU FEEL. THE FINAL OUTCOME IS DETERMINED BY HOW YOU ALLOW WHAT IS NEGATIVELY SAID, TO AFFECT WHO YOU REALLY ARE AS A PERSON! NO ONE HAS THE POWER TO MAKE YOU FEEL BAD, DEFEATED, OR INSIGNIFICANT, UNLESS YOU ALLOW THEM TO HAVE THAT POWER OVER YOU!"*</u> **Remember this for the rest of your Wonderful & Significant life!**

Instructor to the class: Always Remember: Frequently remind yourself and have it ingrained in your mental toughness philosophy: MY DIFFERENCE IS MY STRENGTH!! Refer again to the poem and illustration "My Difference Is My Strength" in last lesson in this training manual. Study and learn the important words, phrases, stanzas, and the poem itself for your Self-Empowerment! (Refer to how a teenage student wrote about the meaning of each stanza of the poem and how he was personally impacted)

These **Techniques** and **WORDS**, along with more to follow, if learned well, practiced, and retained, will give you a much better chance of successfully eliminating and preventing cyberspace and other forms of bullying.

Instructor to Students:

Remember specific phrases and stanzas that send powerful messages to the bully to cease their inappropriate behavior.

Reinforce with Students:

As they read and study the poems, they should make believe they are talking directly to the bully with the **POWERFUL WORDS** in the poem. Looking the bully in the eyes, belief in what they are saying, with conviction, mental toughness, voice inflection, and confidence are all paramount for effectiveness. This should be done, even if they are copying and pasting specific phrases or stanzas as a response to the bully online. As they are doing this their tablet, computer, laptop, etc. actually is the bully — look the **BULLY IN THE EYE WHILE PASTING!**

Instructor to Students:

Your **online response** to the bully will be **unique, surprising, and unexpected**. **Surprise and Confusion** almost always deflates a bully's intent, especially mentally!

- **Instructor Reinforces with Class:** It's highly important for them to clearly understand the main idea or theme of each poem and the same for the illustration, including any hidden messages in the illustration itself.
- **Instruct the Class:** To **critically discuss** the poems and illustrations with their parents/teachers. They should compare their point of view with their parent's/teacher's point of view of the main idea and theme of each poem. Everyone learns with this interaction and open dialogue discussion

Instructor to Students: Study the illustration of each poem carefully before and after you read the poem – there may be hidden messages in each illustration

Enjoy the process while learning the skills and techniques in the Bullies Be Gone! Project. **You will acquire knowledge and skills that currently 95% of all children and teens, no matter their place of residence, DO NOT POSSESS.**

Instructor Reinforces with Class:

In some poems, the **WORDS** of the poem and stanzas will be speaking directly to you, to build your self-confidence and self-esteem. In other poems, the **WORDS** are directed at the bully, telling them with your great confidence to immediately cease their inappropriate behavior! And some poems will be speaking to both you and the bully.

Read the poems often, each time with more **determination** and **conviction** to not be a victim of bullying ever again, or not at all.

YOU MUST EMPOWER yourself with WORDS that make you feel strong and the bully appear to you, and to him or herself, as being **ineffective, insignificant, and weak!**

Instructor: This is an ideal time to take a survey of what you just told the class about 95% of children and teens lacking BBGP knowledge:

Survey:

Ask Class: From what you have learned so far in BBGP training, do you think your friends who have never had this training, know what you have learned in your few weeks of instruction? (The overwhelming response from the class will be, **NO!** My friends DO **NOT KNOW THIS**)

Instructor now poses this question to the class:

Ask Class: Do you think your friends and children and teens in general should have this knowledge and training? (The overwhelming response will be **YES, THEY SHOULD.**)

The Class response to the survey will justify our 95% claim. In fact, 95% may be too low of a percentage. Realistically, it's probably closer to 99%.

HATEFUL WORDS

What is this illustration's theme and what could be the hidden message/s in the illustration?

HATEFUL WORDS

Do you have any idea how much hateful words hurt those kids you're **spewing** them out to?

If you're a bully who uses them, you need to know **they hurt deeply** and could scar a kid for life. Is that what you really want to do?

It may seem like **innocent fun** when you're bullying other kids. The truth is it's not!

If you're a bully, because of the **negative impact** you can have on another kid, you must immediately stop!

I once thought bullying was cool, too, so I would say hateful words to other kids, just to see how they would react.

I would say hateful words to their face. I would say them behind their back.

Then, out of nowhere, I heard the same kind of hateful words, meant for me.

I didn't like it a bit; in fact, I was hurt and angry as can be.

So, I immediately stopped using hateful words. I'm so glad I did.

No one **deserves** to hear hateful words, especially coming from another kid.

Al Johnson

HATEFUL WORDS VOCABULARY: Spewing, hurt deeply, innocent fun, negative impact, deserves

Rumors Online

What is this illustration's theme and what could be the hidden message/s in the illustration?

RUMORS ONLINE

The rumors online about me, coming from you, are lies and you know it.

Are you spreading rumors because you're really jealous of me and this is how you've chosen to show it?

Come on! Is spreading **vicious**, stupid rumors the best you can do?

You're trying to destroy me, but the truth is, in the end, your lies are going to destroy you.

If your intent was to make me feel bad about myself, with rumors spreading all over the Internet,

Congratulations, you **initially succeeded**, but I refuse to go into a **shell-of-shame** because of you. I now **declare** your rumors **meaningless** at best.

You see, my parents and others that care about me have helped me find my **inner strength** that was stuck in quicksand.

I looked in the mirror one day and decided no one can destroy me unless I allow him or her the ability to. Moreover, I should be quite proud of who I am.

So, I strongly suggest you **cease** spreading your rumors and lies about me or anyone else throughout cyberspace.

Your rumors online have no clout anymore. I declare them **baseless** and empty threats. In the real world of decent, good, and respectful people where I live, your rumors have no place.

Al Johnson

RUMORS ONLINE VOCABULARY: Vicious, intent, initially succeeded, meaningless, shell-of-shame, declare, inner strength, cease, clout, baseless

You Hide In Front Of A Computer

What is this illustration's theme and what could be the hidden message/s in the illustration?

YOU HIDE IN FRONT OF A COMPUTER

You're a bully that hides in front of a computer sending out messages of lies, **disrespect**, and hate.

If you must hide in front of a computer to bully me, you're not the **least bit brave** at all. In fact, you're a **phony** and a **fake**.

I actually feel sorry for you as you **hopelessly linger** in your **pathetic state**.

The truth about me or any kid you're bullying will eventually come out. Truth is frightening for you, isn't it? Because **the truth will seal your fate**.

You hide in front of a computer for hours at a time.

Your time would be better spent if somehow you discovered, with other kids, you could become nice and kind.

You hide in front of a computer to go about your **daily sour routine** of bullying other kids.

One day your computer will crash and along with it, your **despicable bullying empire**, too. Just maybe then, you'll feel somewhat sorry for all the **unnecessary** bullying you did.

Al Johnson

YOU HIDE IN FRONT OF A COMPUTER VOCABULARY: Disrespect, least bit brave, phony, fake, hopelessly linger, pathetic state, seal your fate, daily sour routine, despicable, unnecessary

SOCIAL SKILLS TOO

What is this illustration's theme and what could be the hidden message/s in the illustration?

SOCIAL SKILLS TOO

Kids primarily learn academic skills in school.

However, we must teach kids social skills, too.

Kids learn lots of social skills from caring and loving parents as they grow.

Kids need to build on social skills taught in the home. There are real world social skills, too, they must know.

When a kid decides to bully other kids, it is obvious that he/she lacks social skills.

Even if kids aren't bullies, but use profanity and foul language a lot, as so many do, they are lacking social skills.

If a kid is disrespectful to parents, teachers, and other adults, they lack social skills.

It's apparent a kid would not become a bully if he/she had proper social skills.

Learning math, English, reading, writing, and science are all important vital subjects that kids must learn and do.

However, it is just as important for kids to be taught and acquire proper social skills, too.

Al Johnson

SOCIAL SKILLS VOCABULARY: Primarily, obvious, lacks, profanity, foul language, acquire

SOCIAL NETWORK CAUTION

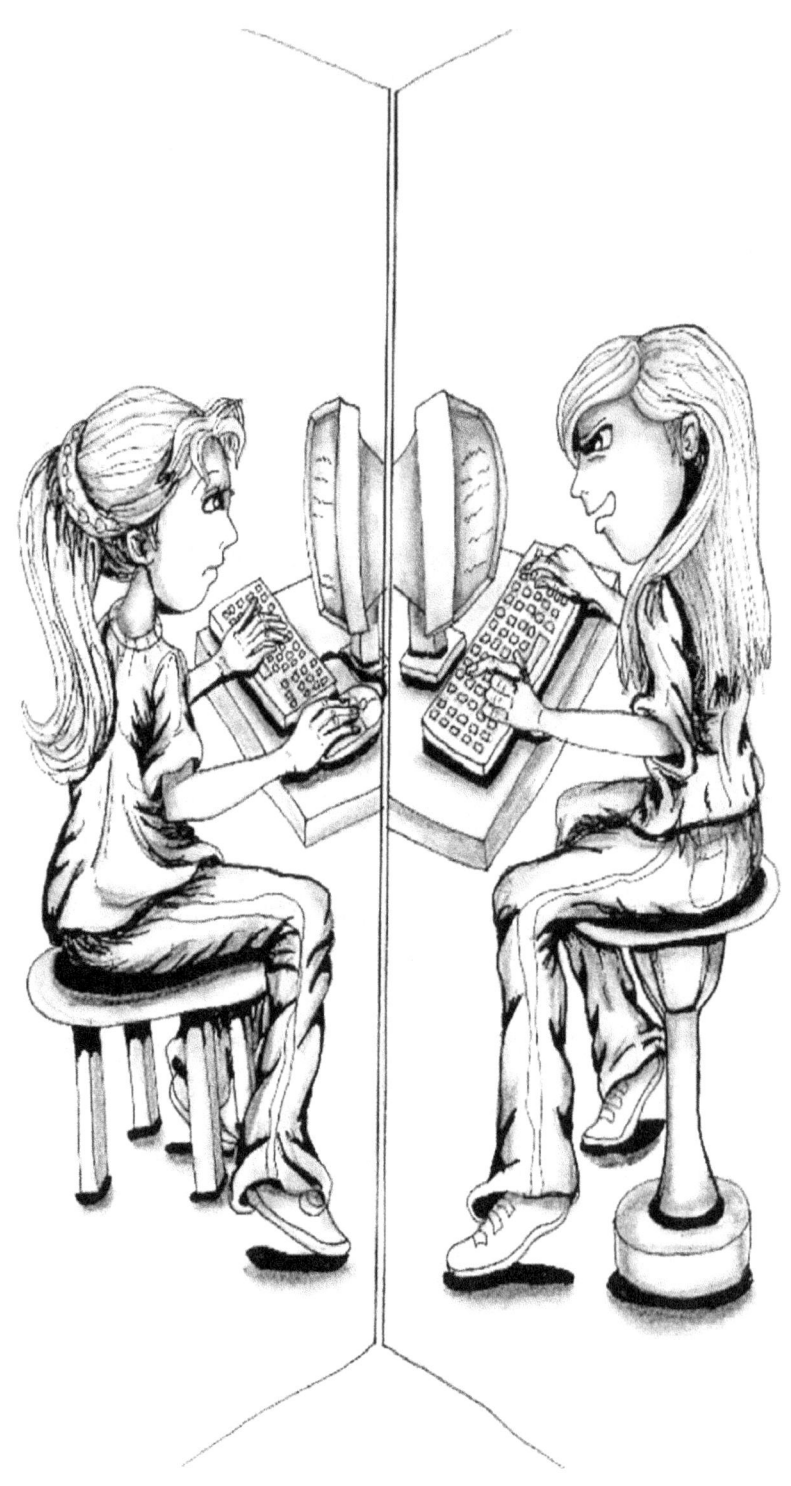

What is this illustration's theme and what could be the hidden message/s in the illustration?

SOCIAL NETWORK CAUTION

Social networks on the Internet are popular with kids, especially teens.

Responsible parents put a block on anything online their children should not hear or see.

Kids you may not like the block, but it's being done because your parents want to protect you.

If you find a way around the block, accessing social networks, be responsible; avoid doing anything online your parents have instructed you not to do.

You'll be **showing respect** for your parents, yourself, and **tremendous restraint**, strength, and **wisdom**, because you may have been **tempted** to.

For teens especially, if you're allowed to go on social networks, **heed your parents' instructions.** People are always online looking to take advantage of a teen like you.

Do not hold conversations in "chat rooms" with anyone you initially meet online. To do so is one of the most dangerous things you can do.

If someone online offers to meet you in person, there are no ifs, ands, or buts to consider; telling your parents immediately is what you must do!

Many kids have been taken advantage of by people they've met online.

Always use social network caution skills when you are online. If you do so, you will be a kid who will successfully make it through your youthful years safe, sound, and absolutely, just fine.

Al Johnson

SOCIAL NETWORK CAUTION VOCABULARY: Responsible, accessing, tremendous restraint, wisdom, tempted, heed, initially, immediately, sound

THE STRANGER ON THE INTERNET

What is this illustration's theme and what could be the hidden message/s in the illustration?

THE STRANGER ON THE INTERNET

The stranger on the internet should be treated just like the stranger on the street.

Parents and responsible adults have told their children never talk to strangers they might meet.

The stranger on the Internet is **constantly on the prowl, looking for any kid they can convince.**

The stranger on the internet knows **slick and enticing ways** to cause a kid to let down his/her defense.

Kids, if you ever come across a stranger on the Internet,

Do not, under any circumstance, chat with them. Conversations with strangers on the Internet can only lead to regret.

Quickly tell your parents or any **responsible adult** about the stranger on the Internet.

Hopefully, you can do this while the stranger is still online.

Then, if the stranger is a bad person that commits crimes against kids, maybe the police can catch him/her quickly. They will then be the stranger on the Internet hopefully, for the very last time.

Al Johnson

STRANGER ON THE INTERNET VOCABULARY: Constantly on the prowl, convince, enticing, regret, responsible adult

Lessons 5-6 Scenario

Instructor to Students: This scenario could happen to you at any time online and when you least expect it — (Use for homework for the class)

To your surprise, one day when you go to school, everyone is looking at you in a strange way, even pointing fingers and laughing at you. You have no clue as to what is going on. This has never happened to you before and the situation is making you feel very uncomfortable. You soon find out the rumors are coming from postings on the Internet on Social Media sites.

To make it more troubling, the rumors are coming from someone you know. You are aware that rumors on the Internet could be seen, read, and heard by thousands of people. This, of course, makes you feel even worse.

Before you answer the following, I want you to be totally truthful as to how you would react to the questions below:

Give you responses to the scenario to your parents, teacher, or Email Al Johnson, with your name and age, or you can bring your answers to the next class session. **(If Applicable)**

If you are emailing your answers, make sure your parents are aware that you are doing so. Get your parents involved; however, your final answers must be yours and not your parents.

Your Name_____ Age_____

Respond with your answers to the following questions pertaining to the Scenario above:

A. How would you handle the situation above if it happened to you or how did you handle it, if it, or if something similar has ever happened to you?

B. What would you specifically say to the person spreading the rumors, if anything, since you know them personally? Would you respond face to face with the person or online? (Hint: Especially now that you have had a few weeks of Bullies Be Gone! Project training)

C. If you know the rumors are not true, which they more than likely aren't, would it bother you at all because of knowing it's false information? Why would it bother you? Or why would it not bother you?

D. If the situation was happening to a close friend of yours, would you get involved to help your friend? Yes? No? If Yes, how would you get involved? If No, why would you not get involved?

E. How would you truly feel with this scenario happening to you? Be candid and tell me exactly how you believe your initial response would be.

Additional writing space

Instructor to Students: For Al Johnson, parents, or teachers to help empower you, please be very truthful with your responses to questions A-E, no matter how you choose to answer. Do not be ashamed of how you might think you would feel with the scenario above. **Any use of profanity, gender or racial slurs, will disqualify you from the training and your parent and teacher will be notified.**

When Al Johnson receives your Email responses, he will Email back to you a critique and ways you have probably never thought of on how to handle the above or similar situations if they happen to you. This should be an overall great learning process. The goal is to give you anti-bullying vital life skills and training 95% of all children and teens DO NOT possess.

Instructor to Students: Learning and retaining the Vital Life Skills Training of each lesson is mandatory to help you prevent or eliminate a bullying problem.

No Meditation Drill (Instructor's discretion)

Instructor Reminds Class: The proper way to practice and study for the best results from The Bullies Be Gone! Project Training

Instructor Mentions Next Week's topics:

Mental & Physical Self-Defense Training (For Escaping & Controlling Only)

Anti-Cyberspace Bullying Continued (Including Role Playing)

Email your responses to: Al Johnson: al@antibullyingexpert.com

END OF LESSONS #5 & #6

Lessons #6 & #7 – For BBGP Instructors, Parents, Teachers, Children & Teens (This will be a continuation of Lessons #5 & #6)

- **Continuation of Cyberspace Bullying**
- **Introduction of Mental & Physical Self-Defense (For Controlling & Escaping Only)**
- **Physical Fitness Warm up Exercises** (approx. 10-15 minutes)
- **Role Playing Scenario for Class & Homework**

Reinforce and Review: Awareness, Hitting "The Light Switch," The 3R's, Mental Toughness, SIC, Body Language, Being Street Smart, Hateful Words, Rumors Online, You Hide In Front Of A Computer, Social Skills Too, Social Network Caution, The Stranger On The Internet, and their importance in BBGP training

Ask Students to Share: Any occurrences during the week since the last class requiring the use of their BBGP skills. Did they witness or were involved in any Bullying situations or potential ones? If there were incidents, discuss same with students. Offer suggestions to make the situation better if a repeated or similar incident occurs. Also get feedback from class.

INTRODUCTION OF BASIC SELF-DEFENSE TRAINING — A person does not have to study self-defense for many years, unless they choose. In today's society, learning basic self-defense techniques that could prevent anyone from becoming an **easy victim** is a wise decision to make for the entire family.

Knowledge of simple, **BUT EFFECTIVE** self-defense techniques applicable to **THE STREETS** should be learning tools for the entire family. These skills are to be used primarily for **Controlling or Escaping** purposes ONLY.

In the following lesson, **Martial Arts Master Al Johnson** will teach you the all-important first steps of applying BASIC SELF-DEFENSE in a PRACTICAL manner.

REAL WORLD SCENARIOS

Al Johnson uses the following lesson in his teachings of private and group classes. Learn and practice the following and you will be off to a good start in learning **PRACTICAL BASIC STREET SELF-DEFENSE that could be effective against a bully's physical intent:**

Lesson 1 — Physical Self-Defense

Instructor Reinforces: Mental Self-Defense is always a component of Physical Self-Defense

Instructor to Students: (Use video demonstration of Self-Defense training by Al Johnson)

What you are now about to learn is Physical Self-Defense skills against a Bully for **Escape** and **Controlling** purposes ONLY.

INSTRUCTOR EMPHASIZES: FIGHTING is NEVER the first choice in the Bullies Be Gone! Project training for eliminating or preventing a bullying problem. However, because 99.9 percent of the time, when a child or teen is being physically bullied, there is NO ADULT on the scene to help, a child or teen needs to know his/her self-defense options.

A push, shove, aggressive grab, blunt instrument strike, or punch to an innocent child/teen can occur within a split second and almost always does.

Instructor to Students: You should know effective ways to escape from or control (if necessary) an aggressive physical encounter with a bully, until a **responsible adult** is on the scene, or notified in some way.

Introduction to Self-Defense: (Power Point and Video instruction)

The following mathematical formula of **Physics** applies to **Physical Self-Defense** in a major way: (Power Point slides and Video instruction)

Instructor to Students: Mass x Acceleration = Force (Demonstrate and Explain)

Knowing how this formula applies to the Human Body and the delivery of Self-Defense Techniques is Critical — Let's break the formula down:

Mass: Is a person's body weight that can be **increased** at the **precise moment of delivery** of a self-defense technique if one knows how to do so

Acceleration: Is the speed in which the self-defense technique is delivered

Force: Is the **impact** of the delivery of the technique

Objective: Students need to learn how to increase the **Mass, Speed & Force** for maximum effect when delivering a self-defense technique.

For Example: Two cars are heading straight toward each other at 35 miles per hour, a head-on collision occurs:

Mass = The weight (**Mass**) of the car x **Acceleration** (35 miles an hour) **Speed** of the car = **Force** = collision, damage at impact

More damage is created at impact if:

The increase in speed is 50 miles an hour (And even more damage, if the vehicle was a heavier one)

This formula is **VERY IMPORTANT** and **KEY TO** generating maximum effectiveness in applying SELF-DEFENSE TECHNIQUES (If necessary & ONLY for Controlling or Escaping)

Instructor Reinforces to Class:
Physical Self-Defense should NEVER be used as a FIRST RESPONSE, UNLESS there is no other choice to avoid physical harm by a bully. This includes the option of RUNNING to escape the scene. ("Emergency Running Skills")

You need to know specific techniques to use against a Bully, if you have no other choice. The skills are designed for you to use quickly, creating the **ELEMENT OF SURPRISE**, which gives you a better opportunity to strike effectively and retreat.

You don't need to and NEVER SHOULD stay around to admire your handiwork. Strike Effectively and QUICKLY RETREAT! (Immediately seek adult attention and help)

How to apply the formula of physics with the human body: (Video demonstration)

Mass x Acceleration = Force

USE OF THE HIP APPLICATION (Power Point)

Practice the following to begin learning how THE USE OF THE HIP WORKS —Applying specific self-defense techniques to the Use of The Hips will be taught.

In almost every major sport, proper Use of The Hip comes into play:

- Boxing
- Tennis
- Golf

- Baseball
- Football
- Martial Arts (MMA, Judo, or Karate schools where the Use of The Hip is a MAJOR component of training)
- Wrestling
- Hockey
- Judo

Instructor to Students: There are others, the above mentioned are obvious— you will understand better after you practice the exercise below.

The Application of Learning to Effectively Use The Hips:

There is a Long Hip & Short Hip — Both are effective and used in delivering self-defense techniques depending on the distance you are from the person you must strike to defend against and escape from.

In this example of using the hip, you will be practicing use of the **Long Hip. The person is within arm's length of you or can be with a quick distance adjustment on your part:**

Video demonstration:

- Stand with your knees slightly bent, your feet about shoulder-width apart, no wider, and your toes pointed inward. **(Not in a pigeon-toed position)**

- Make sure you are relaxed, take a deep breath (**inhale**), and then quickly release the breath (**exhale**) — do this a few times until you feel totally relaxed. (Remember earlier Lessons on **Specific** relaxation exercises)

- Slightly bend your knees, they must not be locked — you are in a position similar to **sitting in the saddle of a horse** — the bending of the knees and sitting in the saddle are for better balance and proper use of your legs. (**The foundation**) You will hear this term often in Boxing: **(He/She needs to sit down on their punches to develop more power. They are boxing too upright)**

- **Your legs play an important role in the Use of The Hips.**

- Don't worry about what you are going to do with your hands (technique-wise) at this point. However, a good habit to form with your hands from the beginning is to **keep your hands high** about mid-face level, just inside your shoulders and your elbows in, not extended out like wings. Make sure your hands are at least the same level of the potential bully in front of you. Preferably your hands are up in a non-intimidating manner, or slightly higher than the bully's hands. Your hands or at least one of your hands should NEVER be lower than the bully's hands.

Keep your hands in this area as you practice the use of the hip. By doing so, you will form the habit of keeping your hands up in a possible close aggressive physical encounter with a bully, who could be throwing a punch at you.

- Now imagine that you are preparing to strike a target directly in front of you. (For example, a person that you now must defend yourself against) Specific striking techniques will be taught in BBGP self-defense training. **The key here is to keep your eyes glued to the target even while your hips are rotating. (Keep your eyes glued to the bully's eyes, never lose eye contact.)**

- Now quickly pivot on the balls of the feet to your left at an angle of about 45 degrees. Then quickly return to the original position you started from. Repeat the same process over and over again.

Your body position when you pivot should be:

Feet and belly button at a 45-degree angle, right shoulder should be pointing toward the person you are striking and left shoulder should be at a 90-degree angle — **you have just practiced the use of the Right Hip**. Remember, your eyes remain glued to the target always. Now practice on the opposite side, so you are using the left hip, everything is the same, but in the opposite direction.

You can also know if your hip is moving properly or not by placing a finger on your **BELLY BUTTON** before you pivot 45 degrees. If your belly button does not move to a 45 degree angle as described above, you did not pivot and use the hip correctly.

- Begin pivoting faster and faster until the process becomes natural. All the points mentioned above must be in play as you are pivoting your hips — practice does not mean to do the drill a few times and quit. It must be done hundreds and hundreds, and hundreds of times, until you lose count — then start practicing over again.

- Once you master pivoting on one side, quickly switch and pivot on the opposite side — rotate over and over again on both sides — don't forget where your hands are, they are up at face level all the time you are rotating your hip and your eyes never leave the target you will be striking. (Unless you have one hand with a finger on the BELLY BUTTON at the beginning of your use of the hip training)

- **You ARE NOT yet delivering a technique.** You are learning how to use and rotate your hip so it becomes natural when you do begin delivering self-defense techniques for Escaping and Controlling against the bully's aggressive physical attack.

Use of the **Short Hip** will be easier to learn, once you effectively learn the use of the **Long Hip**.

Results of the Use of the Hip above: Mass x Acceleration = Force

- **For example:** Your natural body weight is = 180lbs = **Mass (Your body Mass)**
- The faster you pivot your Hip **Coupled** with the **Speed** of the technique = **Increased Acceleration**
- **Results: Powerful Impact = Force**

Instructor Informs Class: What has transpired is without you consciously having to think about the proper Use of The Hip:

Upon impact, you do not weigh 180lbs, your weight was temporarily increased by at least 10%. This makes the self-defense technique you delivered more devastating because you were temporarily heavier than your 180lbs, coupled with the proper use of the hips.

Practice repeatedly until the **Use of The Hip is automatic**. When the application of specific techniques is used with proper hip rotation, you will begin developing Effective and Powerful Self-Defense Techniques for Controlling and Escaping purposes ONLY!

Self-Defense Training for Parent/Teacher will be from Al Johnson's video instruction

The following Self-Defense techniques will be taught in the BBGP Comprehensive training. Depending on the individual class or student, all techniques MAY NOT be taught. QUALITY of learning is more important than QUANTITY. There will be carryovers to future classes:

Self-Defense Techniques to Be Taught: (Power Point)

Teach & Reinforce "Emergency Running Skills" (Video)
- Supported Elbow Frame Block (Prevention of being struck in the head with a blow or blunt instrument)
- Five Most vital areas of the body to strike (There are also other weak areas of the body to strike effectively. They are: **Eyes, Nose, Neck, Groin & Knees**)
- Shoulder Spin Technique
- Shoulder grab from behind
- Escaping from Wall Pin or Tree Pin Situation (Applicable for females, as opposed to males)
- Adams Apple Pinch
- Spear Hand & Reverse Spear Hand
- Claw Hand & Reverse Claw Hand
- Wrist Grabs (Single — Front & Behind), Straight Across, Cross, Double from Front & Behind
- Sleeve Grabs
- Headlock Defense (Pressure points & more)
- Bear Hug Defense (Around the arms & Between the arms)
- Two Hand Choke (Front & behind)
- Rear Naked Choke (The dangers of & and possible Application)
- Arm Bar Technique
- Foot Stomp Technique & Effective street self-defense kicks
- Aikido Techniques & Footwork

Take Home Scenario for Class: (Homework)

The Scenario: You're in team competition or a lively practice session on the soccer field, basketball court, baseball diamond, or football field and during practice, you get hit in the knee, and crumble to the ground in pain. A kid unexpectedly comes up to you, begins calling you a "Wimp," or any other name to make you feel as if you are a "cry baby" or weak, because you are holding your knee in pain, unable to stand up. The kid continues laughing, calls you a "Wimp" again. Some of the other kids begin to join in with laughter also. The coach does not immediately intervene.

Before you answer the following, **I want you to be totally truthful as to how you believe you would react to this or a similar situation pertaining to the questions below.**

If something similar has happened to you in the past, how did you react?

For Al Johnson to empower students, instruct the class to please be very truthful, no matter their response. Students should not be ashamed of how they might personally react to the scenario above. When responses to the questions are received, Al will email responses back with a critique. Al's goal is to give students skills and techniques 95% of all children and teens DO NOT possess.

Students should write responses to:

- How they think they would handle the scene above if it happened to them?

- What would they say to the kid who called them a "Wimp," if anything?

- Would they be the least bit concerned if a kid called them a "Wimp" under the circumstances with a painful knee? Why would it be of concern? If not, Why?

- Would you be concerned about how your peers and friends would react to the situation, since they probably heard the "Wimp" reference and witnessed your reaction or heard about it? If so, why? If not, why not?

- Has anything like this ever happened to you? If so, how did you react then? Would you react differently now? If so, how? If not, why not? **(Hint: BBGP training may now come into play.)**

To the Instructor: Learning and Retaining the Vital Life Skills Training of each lesson is mandatory for a child or teen to successfully Eliminate or Prevent a bullying problem.

No Meditation Drill for this week's lesson, unless instructor chooses to.

Instructor goes over next week's training:

Self-Defense — Scenarios — Cyberspace bullying continued — Role Playing — More educational poetic instruction

E-mail your responses to: Al Johnson: al@antibullyingexpert.com

END OF LESSONS #6 & #7

- Again, if you are emailing your responses to Al Johnson, make sure your parents are aware that you are doing so.

Your name_____Age_____

Your Email address _____

Lesson #8 – For BBGP Instructors, Parents, Children & Teens

Instructor should get in the habit of reviewing previous lessons each time before embarking on a new one.

- Discuss any events with kids since the last class where bullying came into play and how it was handled.
- Quickly review previous important concepts learned in BBGP training.
- Physical Fitness Warm Up.
- Continue with Self-Defense Training.

Instructor to Students: The following important lessons are designed to help you learn effective methods and words of offsetting **hateful and disrespectful words by a bully. Students must Learn effective methods of standing up to the bully with confidence and conviction.**

Poems of Inspiration, Motivation & Training in this lesson: Your Nasty Words Cannot Hurt Me – You Tried To Defeat Me, I Will Not Be Your Victim Anymore & My Difference Is My Strength.

WORDS can Deflate, Harm, Hurt, and Kill — **WORDS** can Empower, Inspire, Build Self-Confidence, Motivate, and Heal.

If a child or teen is **keenly aware** of his/her environment, combined with **being street smart**, those skills alone could be enough to cause a bully to seek an easier victim. Or cause a bully to self-reflect about ceasing their bullying ways.

These techniques, if learned well and retained, will give children and teens a much better chance of eliminating and preventing a bullying problem.

Instructor Reinforces: The Continuation of the Bullies Be Gone! Project recommended instruction for students:

1. Study the poem(s), even memorize some or all the poems for **overall empowerment** and the bully's **overall weakness**. Each poem contains *WORDS* to empower you and offset the effects of a bully's nasty words.

2. Make sure you understand the **main idea or theme** of each poem and illustration.

3. Discuss the poem with your parents and teachers, express your point of view of the poem and illustration, ask them to express theirs – everyone learns by doing so; i.e., what message or messages is/are the poem's author conveying?

4. Study the illustration of each poem carefully before and after you read the poem. There may be hidden message/s in each illustration. What is the illustration saying to you and what does it say to your parents/teachers? See if your parent/teacher sees what you see in the illustration. (This is a great opportunity for **Critical Discussion**)

5. **Enjoy** learning skills and techniques to help you develop effective ways of eliminating or preventing a bullying problem permanently. For this to occur, you must learn, practice, and retain the messages sent with these **poetic *words and other training methods*.**

Instructor to Students: You must be empowered to do this with or without adult or peer intervention. Self-Empowerment!

- As you read the poems, make believe you are talking directly to the bully with the words in the poem. If you ever must say them face to face to a bully, I want you to develop the confidence to do so, if you don't have it now. If your confidence is already strong, I want the words you learn in all the Bullies Be Gone lessons to make you even **mentally tougher and more confident**.
- If the bullying is occurring online, you should cut and paste a poetic response to a bully by using specific powerful lines that apply to the situation.

Suggestion: Copy & Paste 1-4 stanzas at a time to be more effective, rather than the whole poem. (Adding your creative words, could make your response even more impacting and powerful to the bully)

In some poems, the **WORDS** of the poem will be speaking directly to you, to build your self-confidence and self-esteem. Read the poems several times, each time with more **determination** and **conviction** to help you avoid becoming a victim of bullying ever again. You must empower yourself with **WORDS** that make you feel strong and the bully appear to you, and to themselves, as being insignificant and weak.

Some poems will be speaking directly to the bully, sending powerful messages to the bully to immediately cease his/her inappropriate behavior. **Some poems are friend to friend messages, trying to help empower a friend to eliminate or prevent being bullied.**

As before, the instructor will read the poem out loud, while the class follows along silently in their training workbook. Since this is the final lesson, student/s will not be volunteering to learn poems for the Trophy contest. Trophy winners should have been chosen from previous week's performances. (If Applicable)

YOUR NASTY WORDS CANNOT HURT ME

What is this illustration's theme and what could be the hidden message/s in the illustration?

YOUR NASTY WORDS CANNOT HURT ME

You hoped the nasty words you said to me would hurt so much that, like a turtle, I would go into a permanent shell.

My parents told me not to give a bully that kind of satisfaction. From all the nasty words you said, guess what? I'm not feeling bad at all. In fact, I'm doing quite well.

Yes, your nasty words hurt me at first, just as you wanted them to.

I'm lucky to have parents, responsible adults, and even other kids, who showed me how to defeat bullies like you.

I don't care the **least bit** what you do anymore. I really don't care what you say.

Your nasty words cannot hurt me again. You tried putting me down, but with **self-determination** and help from others, I've been lifted in every way.

I see you as a **small-minded bully**, with no positive direction.

I also see you as a kid who could be nice and kind to others, if you decide to change your **intentions**.

Just in case you **refuse** to change and continue with your bullying ways, **declaring** that's just how it's going to be,

I'm going to do all I can to **spread** my knowledge to as many kids as I can. Then the next kid you try to bully, hopefully, will confidently say to you, "Your nasty words cannot hurt me."

Al Johnson

YOUR NASTY WORDS CANNOT HURT ME VOCABULARY: Least, self-determination, small-minded, intentions, refuse, declaring, spread

I Will Not Be Your Victim Anymore

What is this illustration's theme and what could be the hidden message/s in the illustration?

I WILL NOT BE YOUR VICTIM ANYMORE

I will not be your victim anymore, you've gone too far with your disrespect. I've had enough.

You've bullied me, made me cry, and made me sad and mad, too. You enjoy bullying and stuff.

Suddenly, when I woke up this morning, I decided I will not be your victim anymore.

I was surprised how strong I felt just saying those words to myself repeatedly as I walked out my front door.

"I will not be your victim anymore" are words that have a lot of power if kids who are being bullied truly believe.

If kids repeat, "I will not be your victim anymore," it could give a kid the **determination** they need to stop the bullying.

Those words sure gave me strength and confidence; they could do the same for you.

No kid deserves to ever be bullied. If you're a kid and you're being bullied, here's what I suggest you do:

Decide that you're no longer going to be bullied like before.

Say these words repeatedly to yourself, then say them to the bully with **conviction**, when you feel strong and **confident**: "I will not be your victim anymore!"

Al Johnson

I WILL NOT BE YOUR VICTIM ANYMORE VOCABULARY: Determination, conviction, confident

What is this illustration's theme and what could be the hidden message/s in the illustration?

YOU TRIED TO DEFEAT ME

You tried to defeat me with the nasty words you say constantly.

But, instead of your nasty words tearing me down, they lifted me up so I could clearly see.

You're just a lonely bully without any real true friends.

Kids that do hang around with you are just as pathetic, too. I suggest you all find a way for your bullying to end.

You tried to defeat me and probably other kids, too.

For a while, you were successful because I was afraid of you.

But my parents and other responsible adults told me to be confident and strong, no matter how hard it was to be.

They told me this over and over again. One day I was suddenly convinced bullies must prey on weak kids to succeed.

I don't feel weak anymore. In fact, I'm feeling very strong.

You tried to defeat me, it didn't work. From this point on, you had better leave me alone!

Al Johnson

YOU TRIED TO DEFEAT ME VOCABULARY: Constantly, lifted, tearing, pathetic, convinced, prey, succeed

MY DIFFERENCE IS MY STRENGTH

What is this illustration's theme and what could be the hidden message/s in the illustration?

MY DIFFERENCE IS MY STRENGTH

The **difference** in the way I look, walk, talk, or what I **prefer** in life is not my weakness. Because of your **misguided** and **intolerant beliefs**, you need to know, my difference is my strength.

I'm not **ashamed** of who I am. No matter how many nasty things you say about me, my head will be held very high. **My difference is my strength**.

Unfortunately, you must live with your **ignorance and hate**. Unless you change, you'll carry that heavy **burden** for the rest of your **miserable** life.

That heavy load will eventually wear you down. You'll be stuck in quicksand, slowly sinking, as time rapidly passes you by.

You'll never be the good and **kindhearted** person you could have been. You'll never experience the **brilliance of humankind**.

My difference is my strength. I'm happy with and proud of who I am. My strength lies in my heart and mind.

Your **needless criticism** of me and others too, for no **viable** reason, shows how **shallow** a person you really are.

My difference is my strength. Do you even have the **slightest clue** that your nasty tone **unnecessarily**, goes way too far?

My difference is my strength. Your weakness lies in the disrespectful things you say and do.

My difference is my strength. However, you're not a lost cause. I truly believe there's still a **sliver** of hope for positive change, **longing** to come out, somewhere deep inside you!

If somehow, you haven't clearly understood the powerful message to you I've sent.

Emphatically, I say to you again, my difference is my strength!
MY DIFFERENCE IS MY STRENGTH!!

Al Johnson

MY DIFFERENCE IS MY STRENGTH VOCABULARY: Difference, prefer, misguided, intolerant beliefs, ashamed, unfortunately, ignorance, burden, miserable, kindhearted, brilliance, humankind, needless, criticism, viable, shallow, slightest clue, unnecessarily, sliver, longing, emphatically

Below is an example of Critical Discussion & Thinking, Creativity, and Writing Skill's use of the poem My Difference Is My Strength:

A 16-year-old high school student was asked to write responses to the following questions regarding the poem. These are his unedited responses:

Question 1—In your words, with no more than 3 sentences per stanza in the poem, what does each stanza say to you personally?

Question 2—How does each stanza apply to Bullying & Humanity?

Student's Responses:

Stanza 1—My difference is the way I do things and how I live, but you thought it's what's wrong with me.

Stanza 2—I am proud of what I've become. What you say about it doesn't matter.

Stanza 3—You will have to live with your hate for the rest of your life because you don't understand it.

Stanza 4—As you still keep hating of what's different, the rest of the world will move on and you'll be lost of what the world became.

Stanza 5—You won't be a well-adjusted person. You'll never become a good person and you will never understand what the people around you have become.

Stanza 6—I am proud of who I have become.

Stanza 7—Your unreasonable judgment of people reflects the cruel person you are.

Stanza 8—Do you even know how bad of a person you really are?

Stanza 9 – Your drawbacks aren't the person you are, but your cruel beliefs.

Stanza 10—I hope you'll come to understand there's nothing wrong with me and that there needs to be changes in you, your actions, and way of thinking.

Stanza 11—If you still don't know what's wrong with you, unless you listen to people like me, you may never know.

Stanza 12—Simply speaking, there is nothing wrong with me and my traits are innocent and respectful ones.

This authentically written teenage example can be used by instructors, parents, and teachers for each poem in the Bullies Be Gone! Project for enhancement learning purposes and Self-Empowerment, helping children & teens effectively eliminate and prevent being a victim of bullying.

Parent/Teacher can request a Power Point instruction of how to use any poem in the book as a classroom Critical Discussion & Writing Assignment

SUMMARIZE: THE ENTIRE 8-WEEK COURSE WITH THE CLASS

Remind the Class: They have learned Vital Life Skills that should be retained for the rest of their lives.

- What they have learned should never be played with or shown to friends who have not taken this course. (With the exception of the Lesson on Online Anti-Bullying copy and posting techniques)
- Students should continue to review their training workbook and any other BBGP materials at least once a week.
- As students who have completed the eight-week training, they and their parents have continuous access to Al Johnson and any BBGP instructor for follow-up questions or concerns. (Make sure students get the instructor's contact info and Al Johnson's)
- Students should continue to practice all techniques learned in the training at least once a week, if not more, for retention.
- Ask students if they have any questions.

Instructor hands out class evaluation forms to all students to be filled out in class. This should take 20-30 minutes—instructor will collect these forms. We want student's candid opinions of what they felt about the training. With parent's permission, we would like to take video testimonials from students. (If Applicable)

Instructor Tells the Class: We don't want students writing down something they think the instructor wants to hear. We want to know how they TRULY felt about the class and any SUGGESTIONS to make the class even better.

Instructor Hands out Certificates of Completion and bonus gift to each qualified student. Trophies won for poetic performances should also be awarded now. **(Certificates and Bonus Gift can be requested from Al Johnson via Email) Trophies or other inducements will be the responsibility of on sight individual instructors and parents.**

Before dismissing, have the class sit in the Yoga, meditative position, with eyes closed. **They should now silently say to themselves five (5) times**: MY DIFFERENCE IS MY STRENGTH, then individually stand as they have done in previous training sessions.

When the entire class has stood, on the instructor's cue, the entire class in unison **ROARS WITH CONVICTION: MY DIFFERENCE IS MY STRENGTH!!**

Instruct Class how they must practice and review the materials in their workbook to maintain the Vital Life Skills they have learned in The Bullies Be Gone! Project Training!

Parent/Teacher tells students: To remain, Safe, Alert, and Aware

For information on Professional Speaking, Consulting, Additional Training, and Products by Al Johnson, click on the following links:

www.antibullyingexpert.com & al@antibullyingexpert.com

- If students have questions for Al Johnson, they should ask parent/teacher first.

- Al Johnson WILL NOT speak with students without parent/teacher permission

Instructor Reminds Students: To frequently refer to his/her workbook to insure retention of all skills taught.

Instructor Informs Students: They have now completed the Bullies Be Gone! Project 8-Week Comprehensive Training: CONGRATULATIONS!!

Instructor Reinforces: Bullies Be Gone! Project Objective:

Self-Empowerment Training for Children and Teens That Prevents and Protects Against Bullying

Instructor Enthusiastically Announces to the Class: You have now become Self-Empowered!! CONGRATULATIONS!! These are Life Long Vital Skills – NEVER FORGET THIS TRAINING!

Instructor Acknowledges: Thank You to the Parents, Instructors, Students, and Teachers

THIS COMPLETES THE EIGHT-WEEK COMPREHENSIVE BULLIES BE GONE! PROJECT TRAINING